D0466288

JOSEPH MIDTHUN   SAMUEL HITI

BUILDING BLOCKS OF SCIENCE

MAGNETISM

WORLD
BOOK

a Scott Fetzer company
Chicago
www.worldbook.com

World Book, Inc.
233 N. Michigan Avenue
Chicago, IL 60601
U.S.A.

For information about other World Book publications,
visit our website at http://www.worldbook.com or call
1-800-WORLDBK (967-5325).

For information about sales to schools and libraries,
call 1-800-975-3250 (United States); 1-800-837-5365
(Canada).

Library of Congress Cataloging-in-Publication Data

Magnetism.
     p. cm. -- (Building blocks of science)
   Includes index.
   Summary: "A graphic nonfiction volume that
introduces the properties of magnetism. Features
include several photographic pages, a glossary,
additional resource list, and an index"--Provided by
publisher.
   ISBN 978-0-7166-1427-2
   1. Magnetism--Juvenile literature. I. World Book,
Inc.
   QC753.7.M335 2012
   538--dc23
                                2011025979

Building Blocks of Science
Set ISBN: 978-0-7166-1420-3 (print, hc.)

Also available as:
ISBN: 978-0-7166-1469-2 (pbk.)

E-book editions:
ISBN 978-0-7166-1866-9 (EPUB3)
ISBN 978-0-7166-1445-6 (PDF)

Acknowledgments:
Created by Samuel Hiti and Joseph Midthun.
Art by Samuel Hiti. Written by Joseph Midthun.

© Alchemy/Alamy Images 12; © Alvey & Towers Picture
Library/Alamy Images 24; © Jeff J. Daly, Alamy Images
26; © Kevin Foy, Alamy Images 27; © Prisma Bildagentur/
Alamy Images 13; © Peter Dean, Shutterstock 25

Printed in China by Leo Paper Products, LTD.,
Heshan Guangdong
3rd printing June 2014

ATTENTION, READER!

Some characters in this series throw
large objects from tall buildings, play
with fire, ride on bicycle handlebars, and
perform other dangerous acts. However,
they are CARTOON CHARACTERS. Please
do not try any of these things at
home because you could seriously harm
yourself—or others around you!

STAFF

Executive Committee
President: Donald D. Keller
Vice President and Editor in Chief: Paul A. Kobasa
Vice President, Sales & Marketing:
   Sean Lockwood
Vice President, International: Richard Flower
Director, Human Resources: Bev Ecker

Editorial
Manager, Supplementary Publications:
   Cassie Mayer
Writer and Letterer: Joseph Midthun
Editors: Mike DuRoss and Brian Johnson
Researcher: Annie Brodsky
Manager, Contracts & Compliance
   (Rights & Permissions): Loranne K. Shields

Manufacturing/Pre-Press/Graphics and Design
Director: Carma Fazio
Manufacturing Manager: Steven Hueppchen
Production/Technology Manager:
   Anne Fritzinger
Proofreader: Emilie Schrage
Senior Manager, Graphics and Design: Tom Evans
Coordinator, Design Development and
   Production: Brenda B. Tropinski
Book Design: Samuel Hiti
Photographs Editor: Kathy Creech

TABLE OF CONTENTS

There is a glossary on page 30. Terms defined in the glossary are in type **that looks like this** on their first appearance.

MAGNETIC FIELDS

How is it that magnets can pull on objects without touching them?

It's because every magnet is surrounded by a **magnetic field.**

A magnetic field is an area of force around a magnet.

But you can see the effect of a magnetic field by sprinkling iron filings around a bar magnet.

Magnetic fields are invisible.

The filings line up along the lines of the magnetic field.
The lines of the field stretch from one pole to the other.
The lines are closer together near the poles.
This shows that the magnetic field is strongest near the poles.

HOW DO MAGNETS WORK?

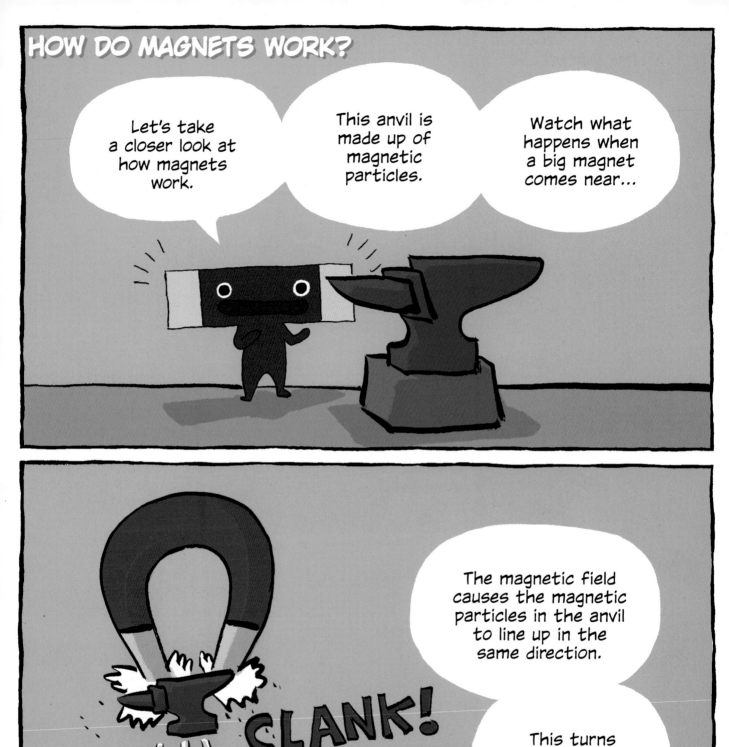

ELECTRICITY AND MAGNETISM

Magnetism is a powerful force on its own, but I'm even more powerful when I join forces with my friend Electricity!

Hey!

Electricity is a kind of energy that people use to run electronics and many other machines.

Electricity and magnetism may seem quite different, but we are closely related.

That's right!

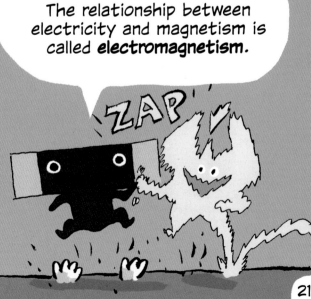

21

An **electromagnet** is a temporary magnet produced by running electric current through a metal object.

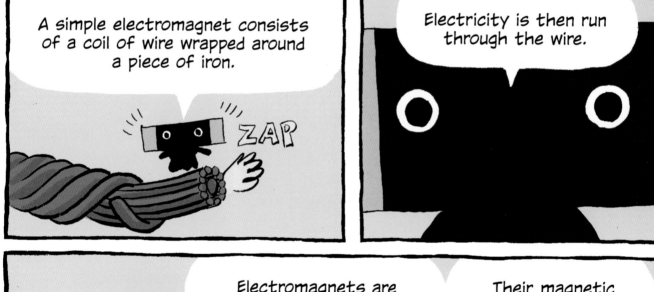

A simple electromagnet consists of a coil of wire wrapped around a piece of iron.

ZAP

Electricity is then run through the wire.

SHUNK

Electromagnets are useful because they form temporary magnets.

Their magnetic fields can be turned on or off!

Powerful electromagnets are used to lift large objects, like cars at a junkyard.

Many machines use electromagnets to work.

Electric generators are machines that create electricity.

They use mechanical energy to create electric energy.

In a generator, magnets and a coil of wire spin around each other.

The spinning produces an **electric current** in the wire.
Power plants use huge generators to produce electricity.
Most generators use steam or water to spin the magnets and wire coil.

Electric motors are used to power such machines as blenders, fans, and vacuum cleaners.

Like generators, electric motors use magnets and coils of wire.

But unlike generators, they use electric energy to create mechanical energy.

In an electric motor, electric current turns on a set of electromagnets, creating a magnetic field.

The magnetic field forces the coil of wire to spin.

VRRRRR

In some parts of the world, you can ride on trains that float above the train tracks!

These trains are called maglevs. They use magnetic **repulsion** to move along the tracks.

Magnets on the bottom of the train and on the tracks repel each other.

Remember how hard it was to push the same poles on two magnets together?

By angling the magnets, the train can move forward!

GLOSSARY

attract to pull one object toward another.

distance the amount of space between two points.

electric current a steady flow of electrons through a material, most commonly a metal.

electric generator a machine that produces electric power from mechanical energy (motion).

electric motor a machine that produces mechanical energy (motion) from electric power.

electromagnet a temporary magnet produced by the flow of an electric current.

electromagnetism the relationship between electricity and magnetism.

force a push or a pull.

magnetic field an area of force around a magnet.

magnetism a force produced by the motion of electrons (negatively charged particles) in a material.

metal any of a large group of elements that includes copper, gold, iron, lead, silver, tin, and other elements that share similar qualities.

pole one of two poles of a magnet. Magnetic fields are strongest near magnetic poles.

repel to force apart or away.

repulsion the action of repelling or condition of being repelled.

speed the distance traveled in a certain time.

universe everything that exists everywhere, including Earth, the stars, planets, and other heavenly bodies.

FIND OUT MORE

Books

Attract and Repel: A Look at Magnets by Jennifer Boothroyd (Lerner Publications, 2011)

Experiments with Magnets by Salvatore Tocci (Children's Press, 2001)

Magnet Power! by Shar Levine and Leslie Johnstone (Sterling Publishing, 2006)

Magnets: Pulling Together, Pushing Apart by Natalie M. Rosinsky and Sheree Boyd (Picture Window Books, 2003)

Magnetism by John Farndon (Benchmark Books, 2002)

Magnetism and Magnets by Michael Flaherty and Ian Moores (Copper Beech Books, 1999)

The Science of Magnets by Jonathan Bockneck (Gareth Stevens Publishing, 2000)

What Is Electricity and Magnetism? by Richard Spilsbury and Louise Spilsbury (Enslow Elementary, 2008)

Websites

BBC Schools Science Clips: Magnets and Springs
http://www.bbc.co.uk/schools/scienceclips/ages/7_8/magnets_springs.shtml
Play around with magnets—and other physics concepts—in this online game from the BBC.

Electromagnet
http://www.sciencebob.com/experiments/electromagnet.php
Build your own electromagnet (with adult supervision!) at Science Bob's science education website.

Exploratorium: Science Snacks About Magnetism
http://www.exploratorium.edu/snacks/iconmagnetism.html
Quick and easy experiments turn everyday objects into physics lessons at this website.

Fact Monster: Magnetism
http://www.factmonster.com/ce6/sci/A0831162.htmlScience
Get the basics about electricity and magnetism, as well as some more advanced details, at this educational website.

Kids' Magnet and Magnetism Experiments
http://www.kids-science-experiments.com/cat_magnetic.html
Build, test, and have fun with magnets using these online experiments.

NeoK12: Magnetism
http://www.neok12.com/Magnetism.htm
Videos at this site take you through the science and uses of magnets and electromagnets.

Physics4Kids: Electricity and Magnetism
http://www.physics4kids.com/files/elec_intro.html
Take a closer look at how magnets work at this educational website.

INDEX